Howard Hodgkin Stage Designs

Howard Hodgkin
Stage Designs

Anthony d'Offay
2002

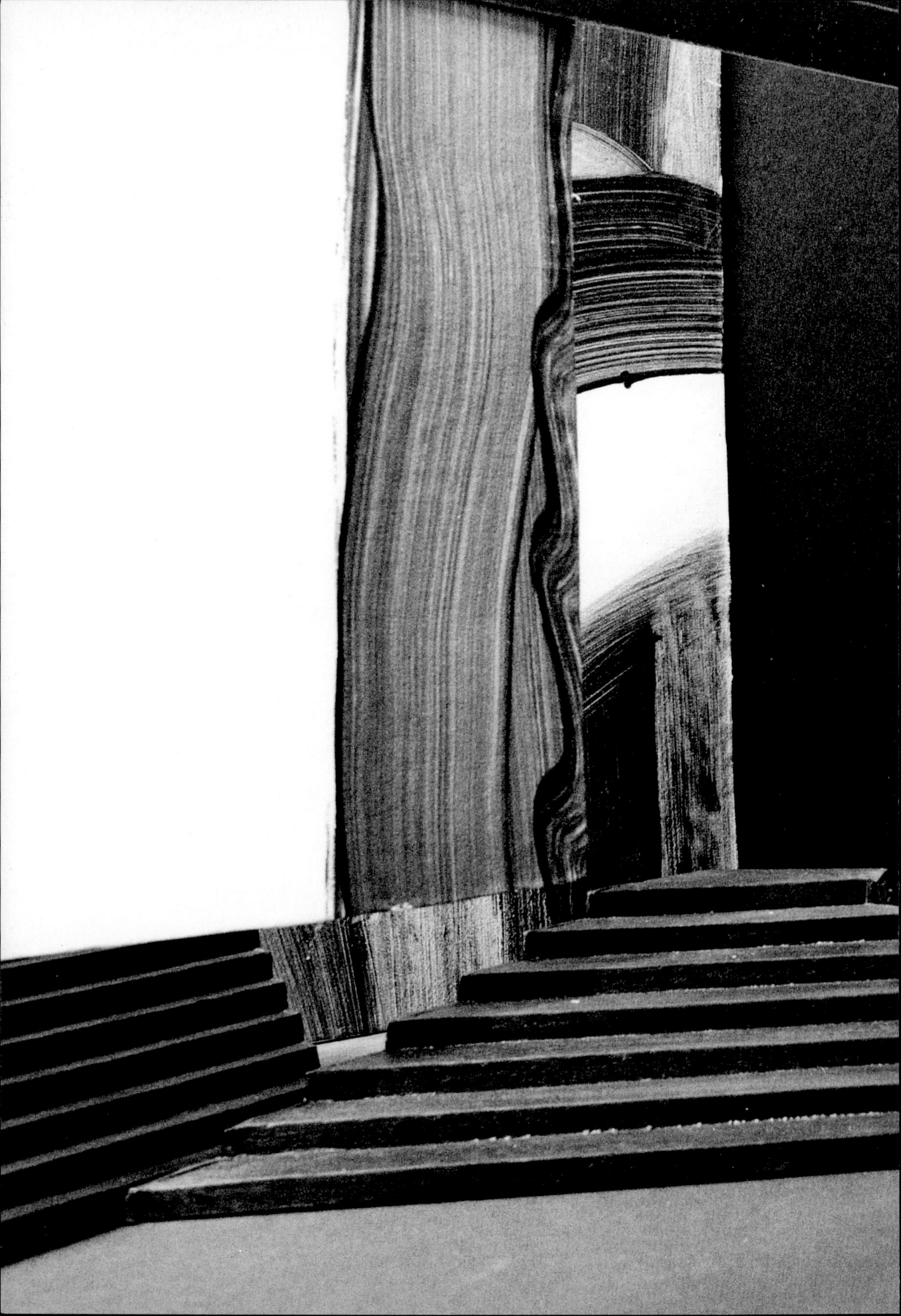

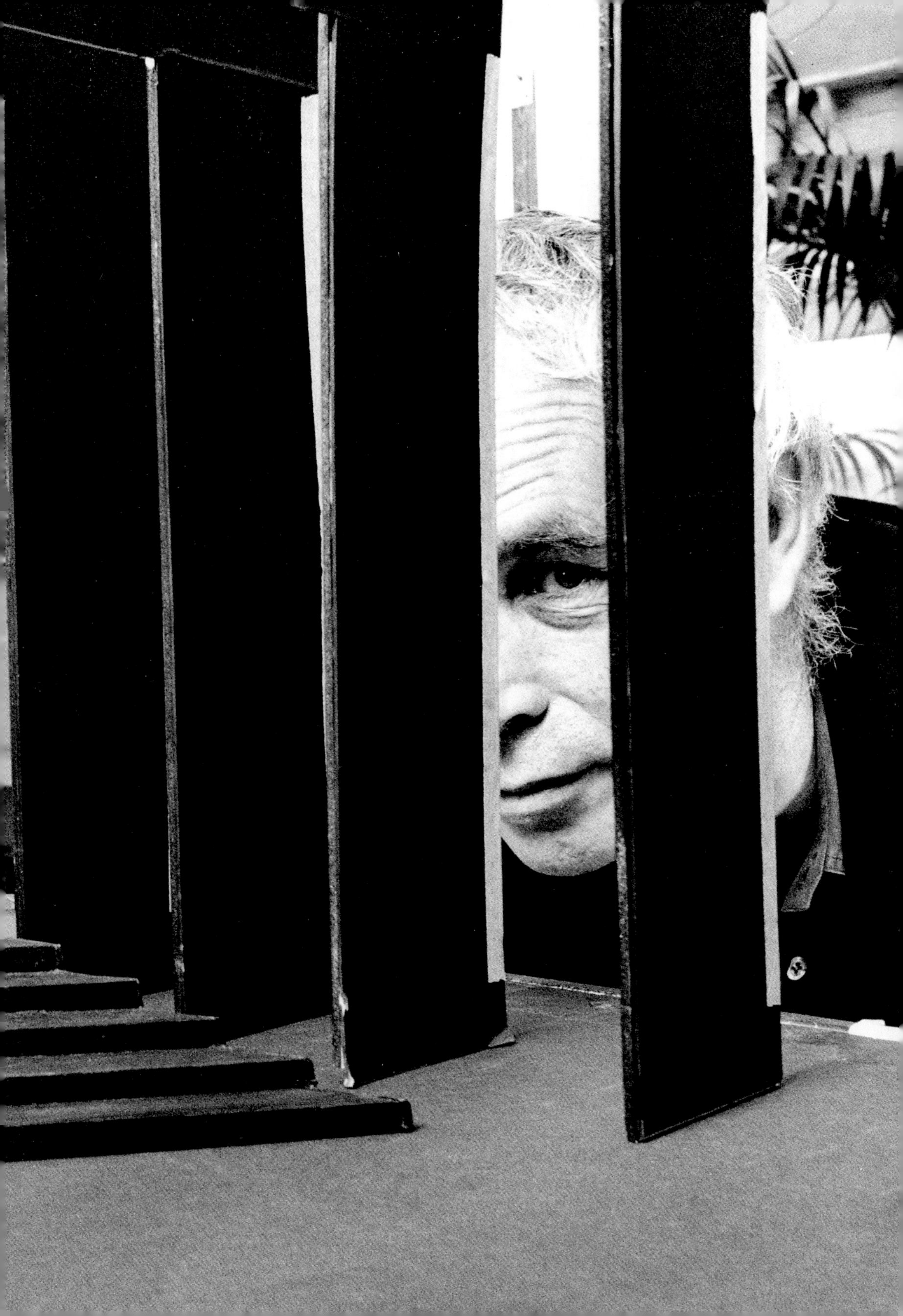

Howard Hodgkin Stage Designs

The desire to unify sounds, images, movement and words finds its natural place on the theatrical stage. Collaborations between painters, sculptors, choreographers, composers and writers benefit not only from the box and frame of a theatre, but also from the freedom and experimentation granted by working with established, classical forms such as ballet and opera. There is, of course, a long history of this type of multimedia experience that can be traced back not just to Wagner's Bayreuth, but further to the combination of decoration and ritual in the church, when painting and sculpture were central to the performance of religious ceremonies and festivals. The more the arts became distinguished from one another in the modern world, however, the more they needed an artificial, deliberately magical setting in which they could be reunited. Certain figures stand out: Serge Diaghilev was certainly familiar with Wagner's idea of *Gesamtkunstwerk*, reinterpreting it in the 1910s and 20s, in Europe and America, with the *Ballets Russes,* and involving the in-put of painters such as Picasso, Derain, Matisse, Gris and Braque. At almost the same time in Germany, Oskar Schlemmer was pioneering extraordinary collaborative performances at the Bauhaus. The theatre was highly important for artists during this period of avant-garde experimentation, forming the public space in which many seminal ideas were developed.

After World War II, John Cage and Merce Cunningham famously worked with Robert Rauschenberg, Jasper Johns and Andy Warhol. In the 1970s and 80s the idea of collaboration between artists and the theatre was given renewed impetus. An important figure for this movement in Britain was the art writer and gallery director Bryan Robertson, who was instrumental in setting up many collaborations, including artists such as Alan Jones, John Hoyland and Christopher le Brun. It was Robertson who introduced Howard Hodgkin to Richard Alston, then director of the Rambert Dance Company (The Ballet Rambert, as it was known until 1987, was established by Marie Rambert in 1926, establishing a direct link with Diaghilev's *Ballets Russes*, for whom she had danced.) The result of this meeting was the 1981 dance *Night Music*, choreographed by Richard Alston with costume and set designs by Howard Hodgkin.

Since this first professional excursion into the theatre, Hodgkin has produced set and, in three cases, costume designs for a total of seven different ballets, dances and operas. There is a strong and not completely unfounded temptation to see a direct relationship between these designs and his paintings. Many of his works have an enclosed, intimate and magical quality that evokes the space of the theatre, thick swathes of paint suggesting scenery drops, curtains or the proscenium arch. His sensibility and his particular touch, his very personal manner of putting paint on wood, seem to transfer naturally to the stage.

However, it becomes clear in an exhibition context that Hodgkin's stage designs should be placed in a different category. Before anything else they are images that must contain the potential for further transformation. The transformations that are fully worked through in a painting; paint into light, paint into flesh, are not needed here. When hung in a gallery Hodgkin's paintings need a great deal of space to themselves in which to glow and live their distinct lives. Sets by comparison, exist at very close quarters with all manner of other expressive activities, and therefore require, to a degree, the effacement of artistic personality; a delicate and diplomatic holding-back, a mutual respect. The same goes for dancers, singers and musicians. But what is held back is held back in the interests of a greater good: personality is transmuted into something more valuable. This distinction is an important one, and one which Hodgkin is very aware of. His use of collage in certain designs, a 'de-personalised' technique found very rarely in his work, underlines the difference.

The nature of his collaborations has varied from production to production. For both works made for the Ballet Rambert, *Night Music* (1981) and *Pulcinella* (1987), and for the Royal Ballet production *Piano* (1989), Hodgkin had a close working relationship with the production team as the work developed. The collaboration with Richard Alston and Ballet Rambert was particularly close and fruitful. Alston had chosen the music for *Night Music* – Mozart's *Notturni and Divertimenti*, for its relation to the intimate social nature of Hodgkin's paintings, evident in his portraits of friends or pictures based on memories of people and places. For the second scene of *Pulcinella*, in which his rivals assail Pulcinella at night, Hodgkin's glowing moon design recalls his small painting *The Moon* (1978–80), with which Alston was familiar. For both productions Hodgkin designed costumes after attending rehearsals and seeing the way that the dancers moved and the way they communicated the story. His designs for these are characterised by their unmistakeably Hodgkinesque colour, as well as the close attention paid to details such as the width of shoulder straps.

By comparison, his work for the Mark Morris Dance Group, *Rhymes with Silver* (1997) and *Kolam* (2002), as well as the Smithsonian Institute's production of Holst's *Sāvitri* (1999) was made at a greater distance, the collaboration depending more on the music to provide a bridge between designing the backdrop and the choreography of the dance. Here the designs result from the artist's own response to the music. The choreography and production beginning with the design as a given. In yet another category, *The Orphanage, The Land of Snow* and *The Land of Sweets* are three designs for Matthew Bourne's adaptation of *The Nutcracker*, performed at the 1992 Edinburgh Festival, that were eventually not used. In this case we are left with fragments without a whole and have to make the creative leap ourselves in imagining how these designs could have been used.

Theatre designs have a valuable afterlife. When the performance has completed its run they appear as fragments and remnants, difficult objects, nostalgic, vagrant, with the sadness of past magic about them. Their importance, however, is that they are preserved in a way that the actual set and costumes are not. These are used-up in performances, recycled, worn-away, eaten by moths while in storage, or just lost. The original designs also retain an authenticity that is impossible to capture with photography. An exhibition of these works therefore serves a double purpose; to document performances and to show fascinating objects that have a memory; witnesses to a particular creative moment.

John-Paul Stonard

Stage Designs

Night Music 1981

This dance was based on a selection of Mozart's *Notturni and Divertimenti*, composed to be played to an intimate circle of friends at evening parties. The dancers arrive in three groups of three and the story unfolds through situations of attachment, jealousy and estrangement. The relations between the dancers are expressed through the combination of formal eighteenth-century court dance patterns and a type of movement described by the choreographer Richard Alston as, comparatively, 'ecstatic, uninhibited'. The story evolves in three parts, the first and last against a deep pink drop curtain, flanked by brown curtains and silver-foil panelled wings that reflected the entrances and exits of the dancers. This curtain lifts for the second part to reveal a richly coloured design incorporating collaged patterned paper and large smudged paint marks.

First performed by Ballet Rambert at the Theatre Royal, Newcastle on 9 October, 1981.

Choreography	Richard Alston
Set and costume design	Howard Hodgkin
Music	W. A. Mozart
	Six Notturni for voices and basset horns, and movements from divertimenti for basset horns
Lighting	Peter Mumford
Photo of performance	Anthony Crickmay
	Courtesy Ballet Rambert and V&A Picture Library

Back cloth design for *Night Music*, 1981
Water based paint and collage on paper, 30.9 × 45.8 cm / 12 1/8 × 18 ins

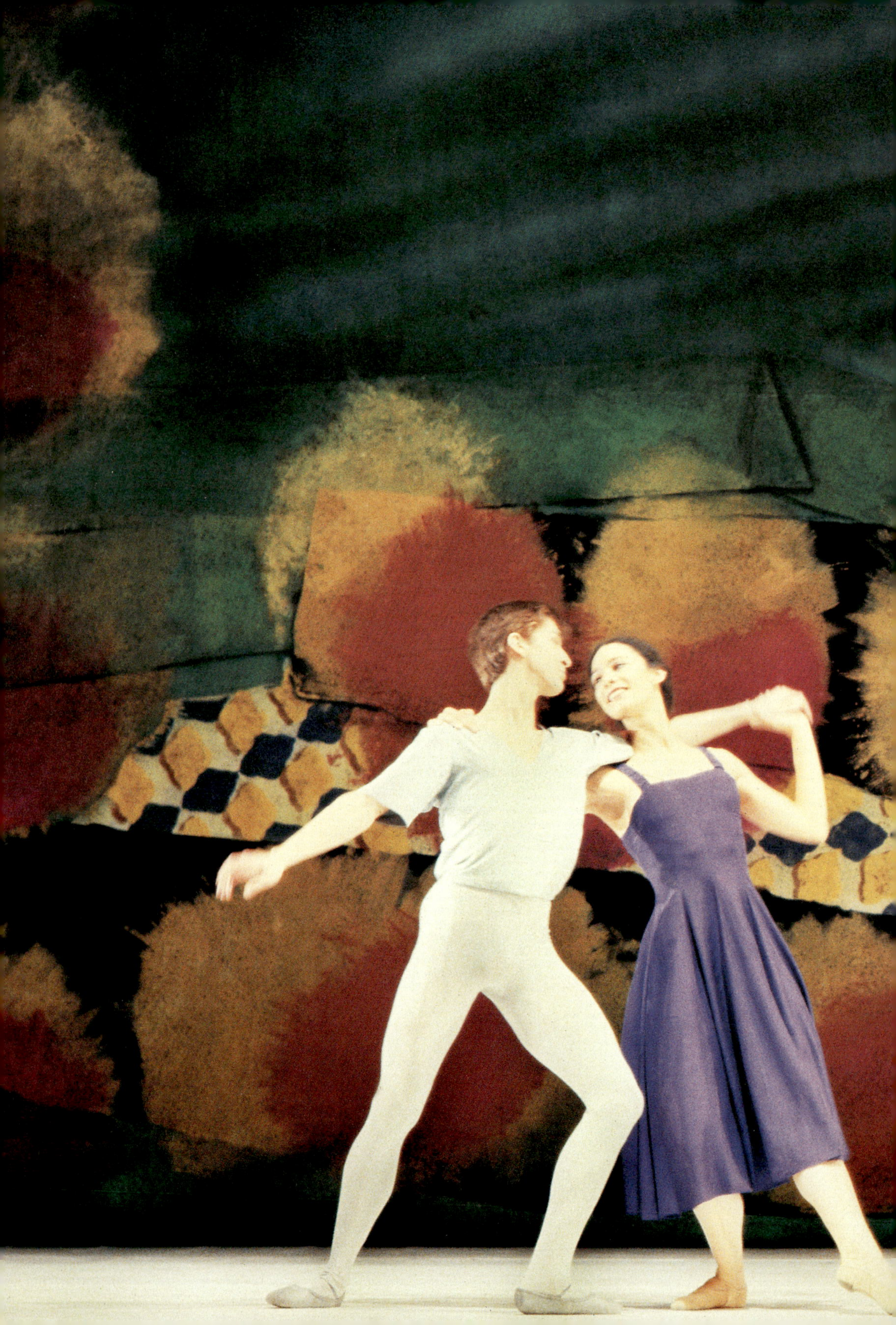

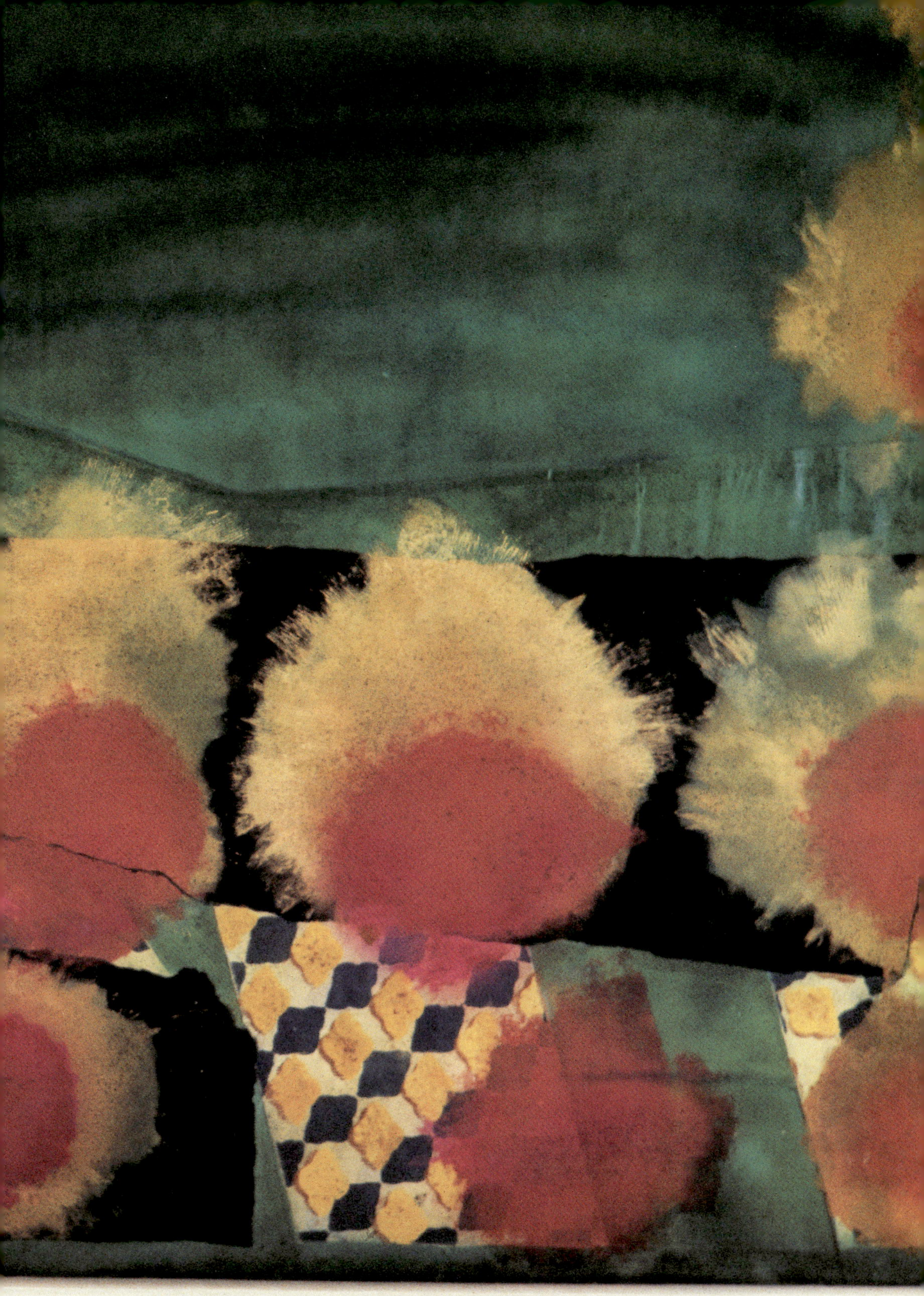

Pulcinella 1987

Hodgkin's work for Pulcinella comprises perhaps the most strongly referential of his stage designs. However these references are not to the *commedia dell'arte* origins of the composition that were prominent in the first production, choreographed by Leonide Massine with designs by Picasso, for Diaghilev's *Ballets Russes* in 1920. Rather, Hodgkin evokes Neopolitan settings in a more general sense. Heavy classical rustication in the first act, a huge glowing Mediterranean moon in the second and an animated carnival with flags, including the red, white and green of the Italian flag, in the third. His designs evoke both the light and colour of Naples and the excitement and sense of the story. The characters in the ballet — Pulcinella, Pimpinella, lovers, friends and neighbours, are distinguished by Hodgkin's costume designs, the changes aiding the telling of the story. The first two scenes use single coloured costumes, bright for the lovers, subdued for the friends and neighbours, and then patterned costumes in the last scene. Pulcinella and Pimpinella wear white costumes until the final scene, when Pimpinella's shoulder straps change from red to black, and her underskirt, stockings and shoes from white to black.

First performed by Ballet Rambert at the Leeds Grand Theatre on 13 January 1987. Thirty-nine stage performances around Britain, ending in London, Sadler's Wells Theatre, May 1988.

Choreography	Richard Alston
Set and costume design	Howard Hodgkin
Music	Igor Stravinsky after Giambattista Pergolesi, 1920
Lighting	Peter Mumford
Photo of performance	Catherine Ashmore
	Courtesy Ballet Rambert

Back cloth design for Act I of *Pulcinella*, 1986
Gouache and collage on paper, 30.5 × 56.5 cm / 12 × 22¼ ins

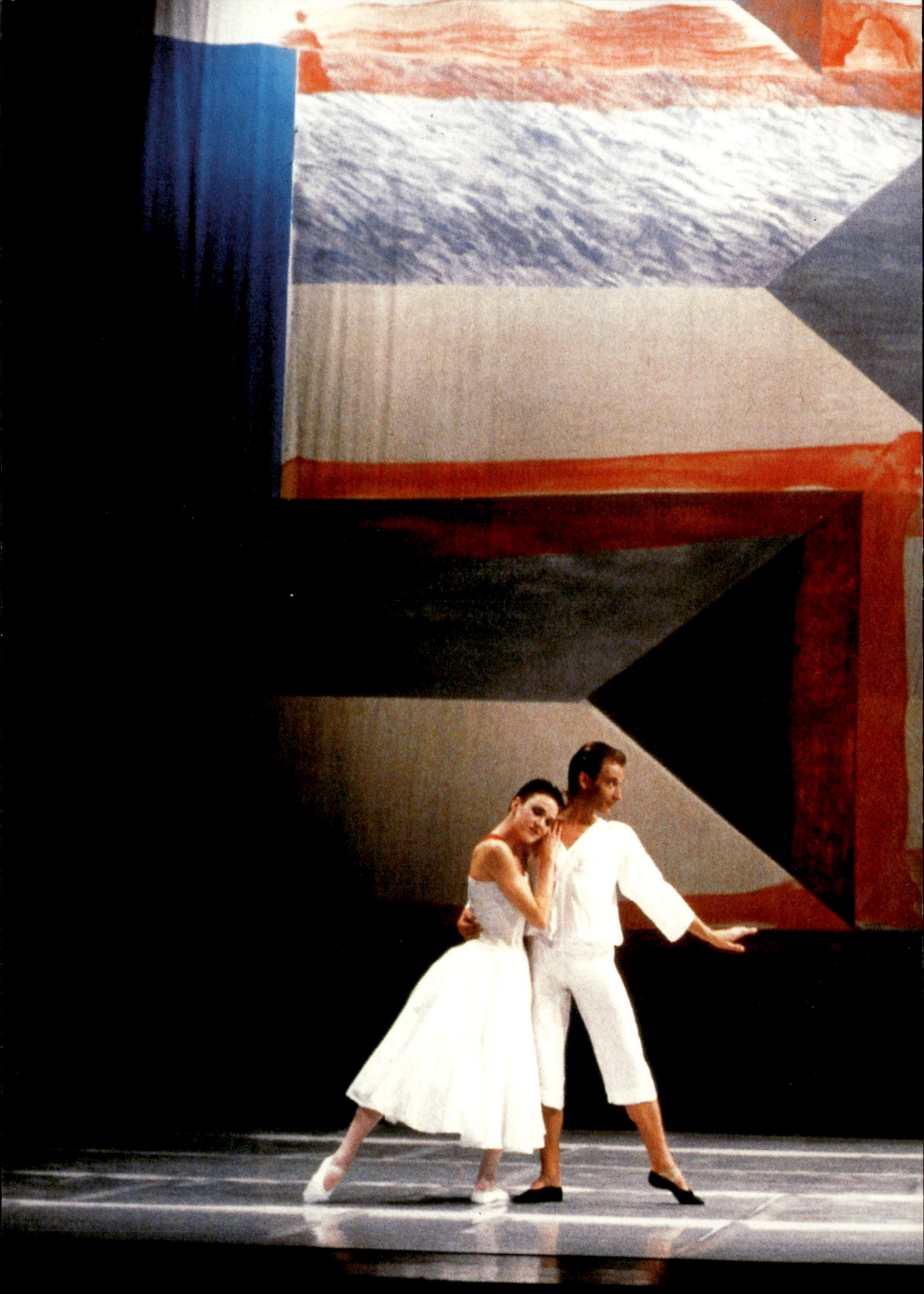

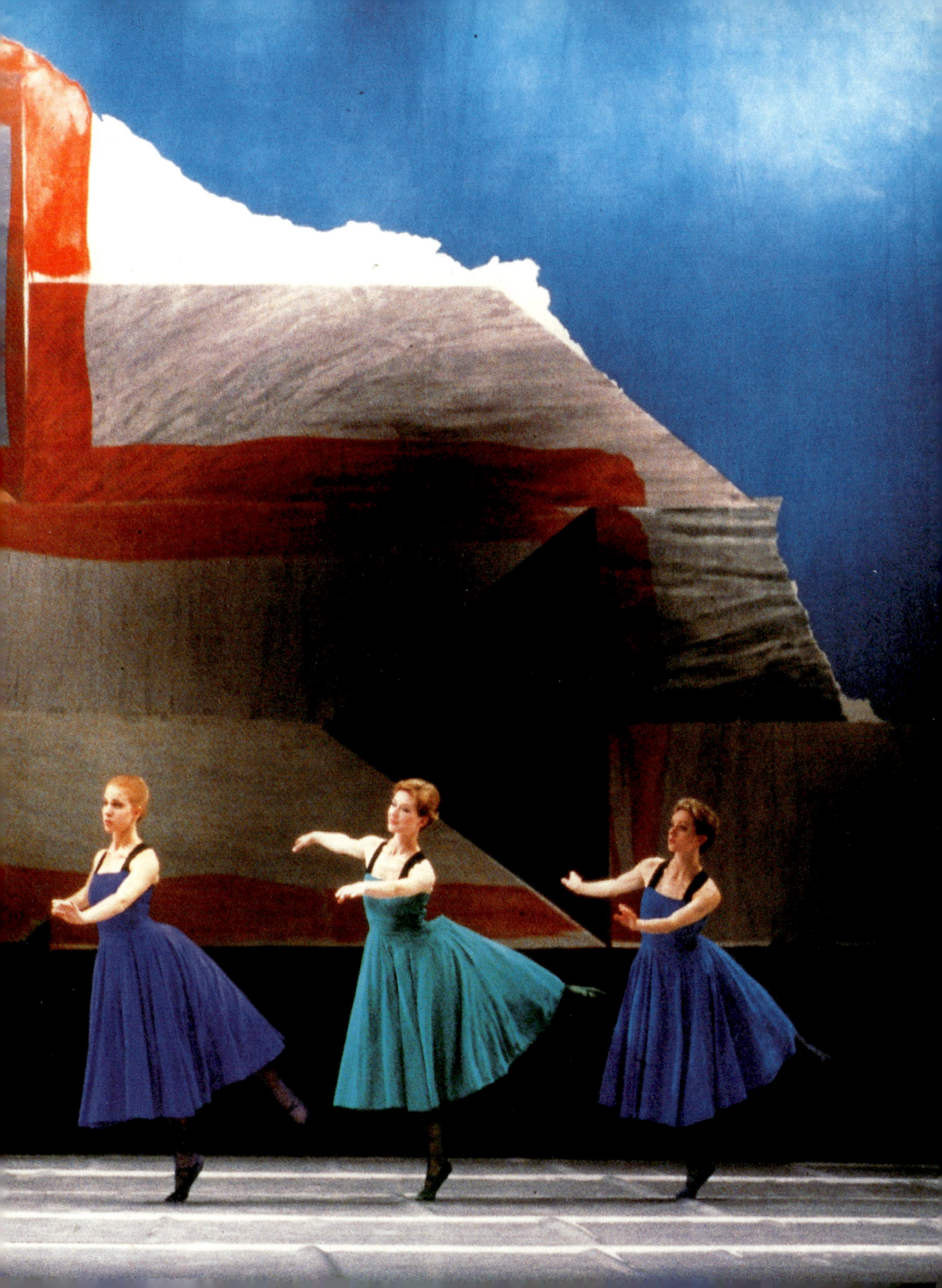

Back cloth design for Act II of *Pulcinella*, 1986
Gouache and collage on paper, 30.5 × 56.5 cm / 12 × 22¼ ins

Back cloth design for Act III of *Pulcinella*, 1986
Gouache and collage on paper, 30.5 × 56.5 cm / 12 × 22¼ ins

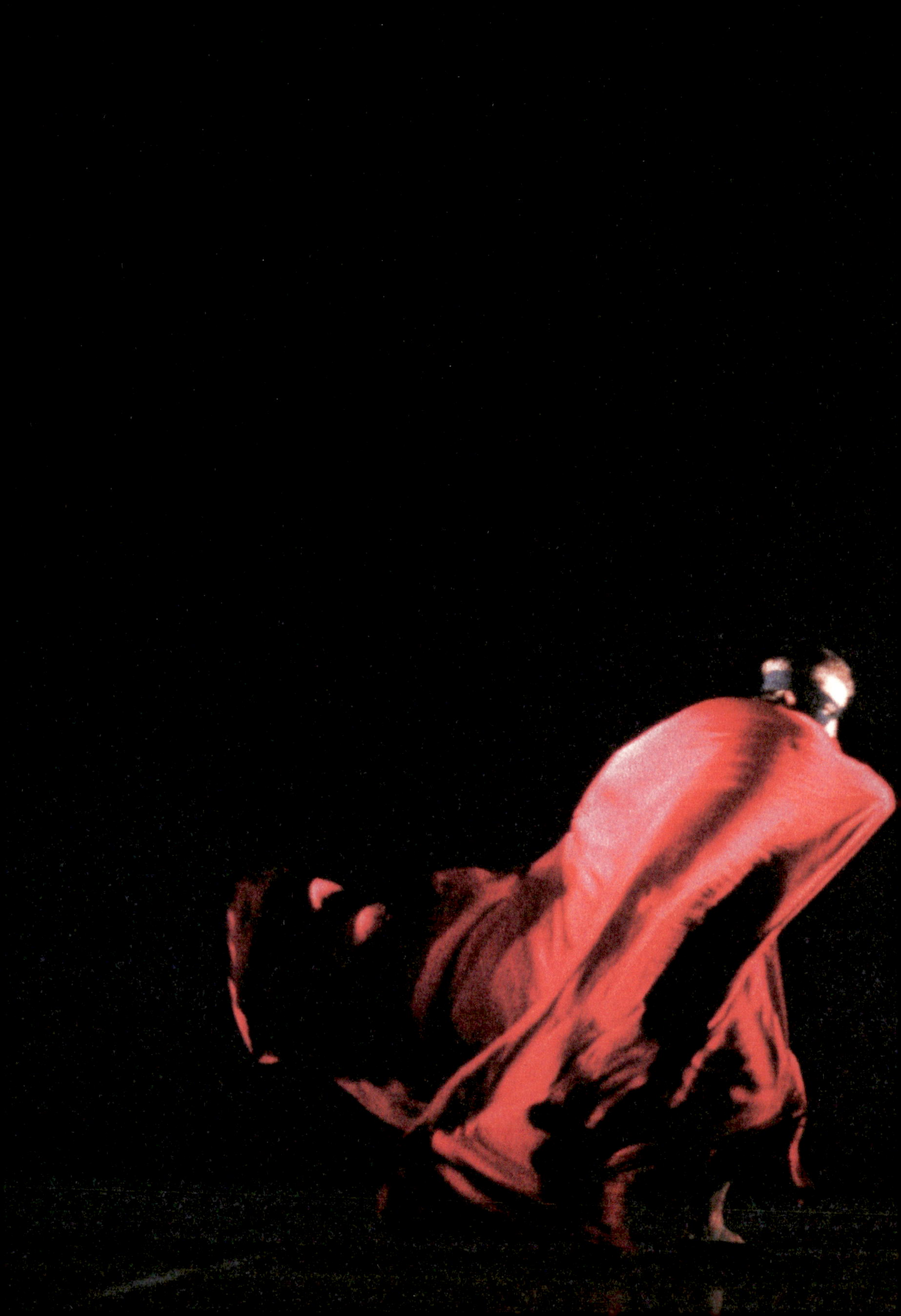

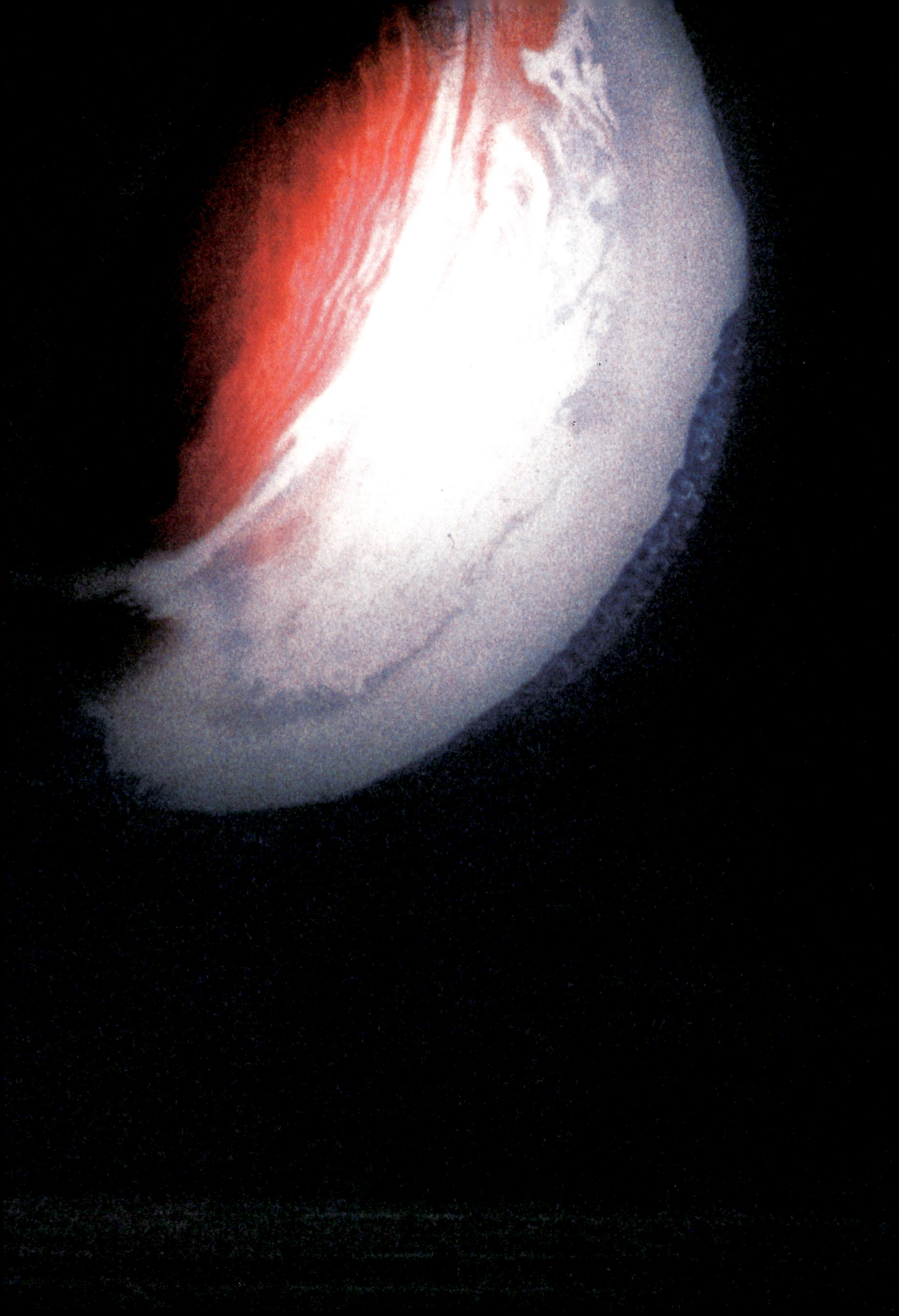

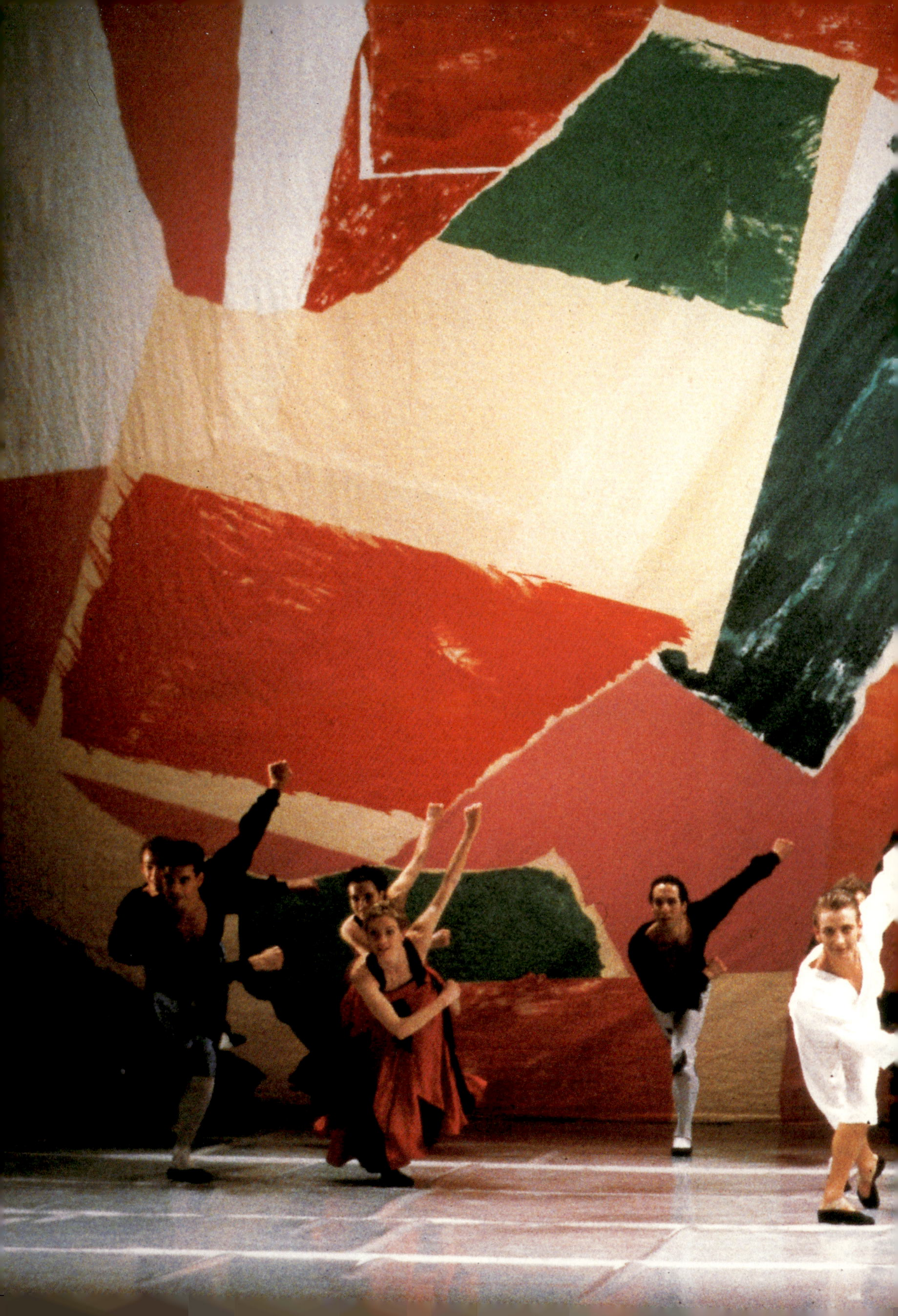

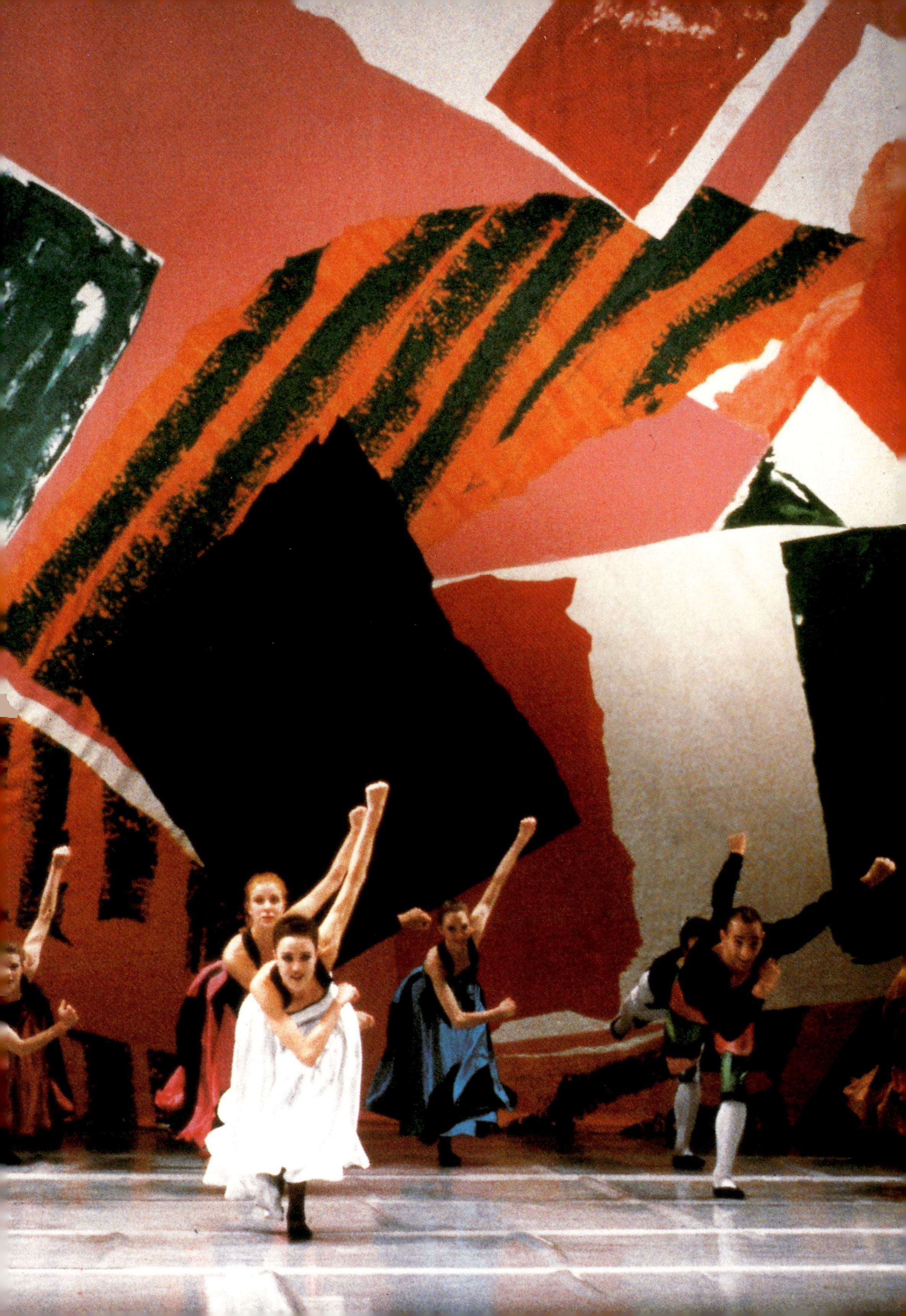

Piano 1989

Taking Beethoven's first Piano Concerto as the starting point, Ashley Page choreographed *Piano* for the Royal Ballet in close collaboration with Hodgkin. As Page has said: 'I invited Howard to design the ballet for a clear and simple reason. All of his paintings embrace at once a most concise formal design and are also often concerned with intimate personal situations.' As well as an exuberant backdrop that was gradually revealed throughout the piece, Hodgkin designed the costumes for both the five principals and the corps de ballet.

First performed by the Royal Ballet at the Royal Opera House Covent Garden on 6 October 1989.

Choreography	Ashley Page
Set and costume design	Howard Hodgkin
Music	Ludwig van Beethoven
	Concerto Number 1 in C Major for Piano and Orchestra, Opus 15. Conducted by Isaiah Jackson
Photo of performance	Catherine Ashmore
	Courtesy Royal Ballet

Back cloth design for *Piano*, 1989
Oil on paper mounted on board, 45.7 × 55 cm / 18 × 21⅝ ins

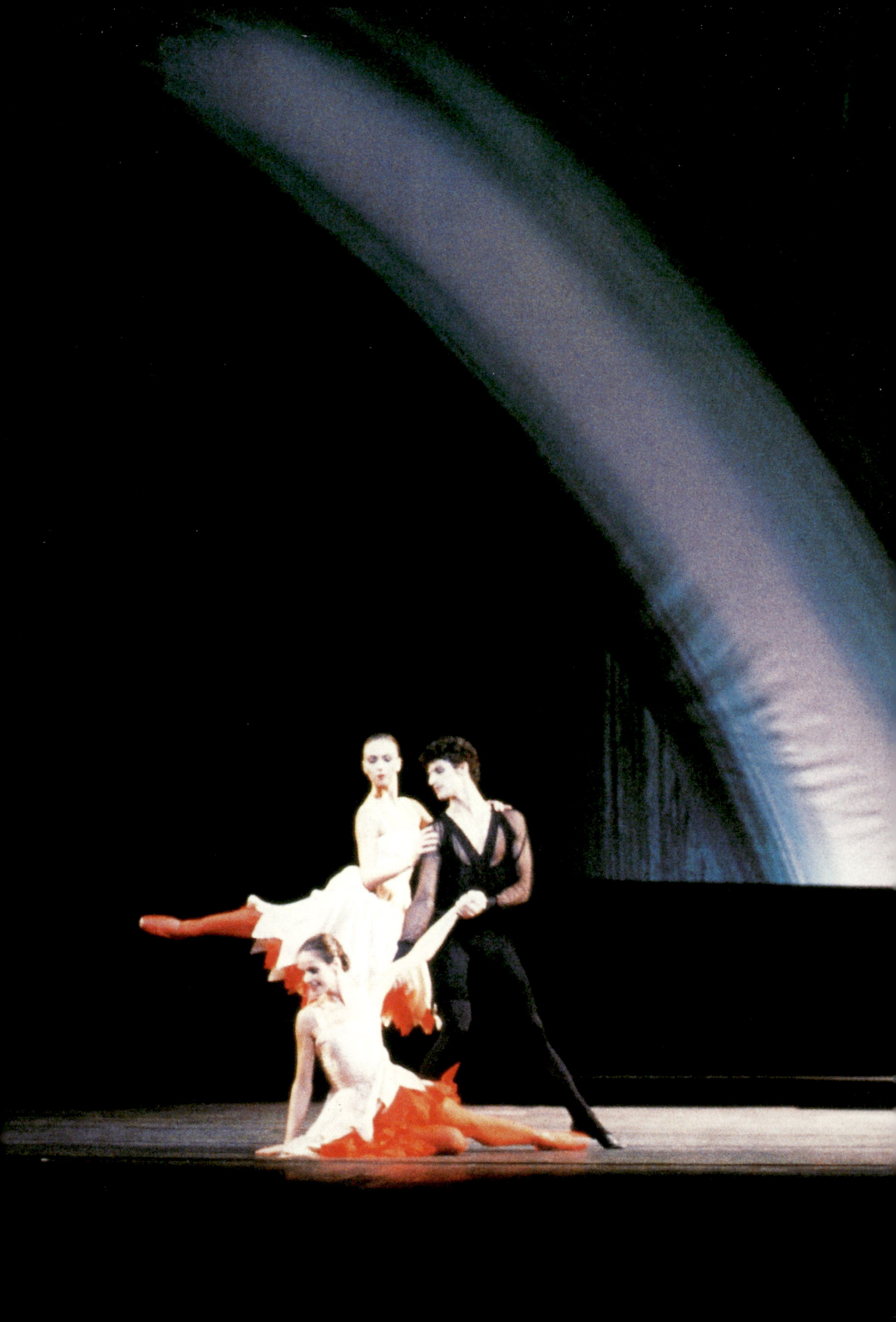

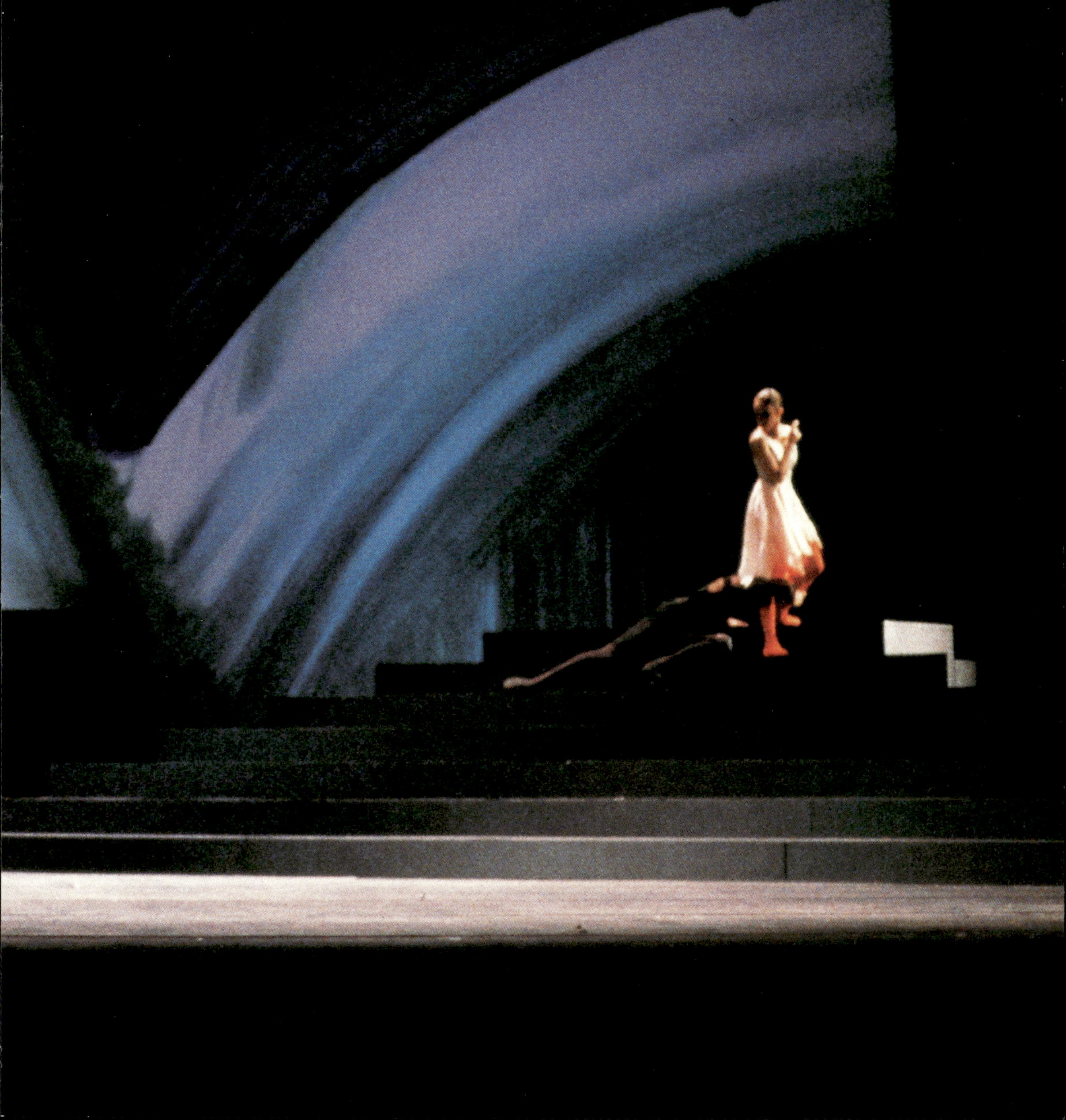

Rhymes with Silver 1997

Mark Morris is generally recognised as one of the world's foremost choreographers. After a highly successful early career as a dancer, he founded the Mark Morris Dance Group in 1980. While acting as Director of Dance at the Théâtre Royal de la Monnaie in Brussels (1988–91) he worked with the choreographer Mikhail Baryshnikov and co-founded the White Oaks Dance Project. Morris has also worked extensively in Opera. *Rhymes with Silver* was performed with original music by Lou Harrison, as part of a series of productions with the cellist Yo-Yo Ma. Hodgkin's backdrop for this dance is a simple stack of red and green waves, designed to change dramatically under differing lighting conditions.

First performed by the Mark Morris Dance Group at Zellerbach Hall, University of California, Berkeley on 6 March, 1997.

Choreography	Mark Morris
Set design	Howard Hodgkin
Costume design	Martin Pakledinaz
Music	Lou Harrison
Lighting	Michael Chybowski
Photo of performance	Ken Friedman
	Courtesy Mark Morris Dance Group

Back cloth design for *Rhymes with Silver*, 1997
Gouache on card, 29.2 × 50.8 cm / 11½ × 20 ins

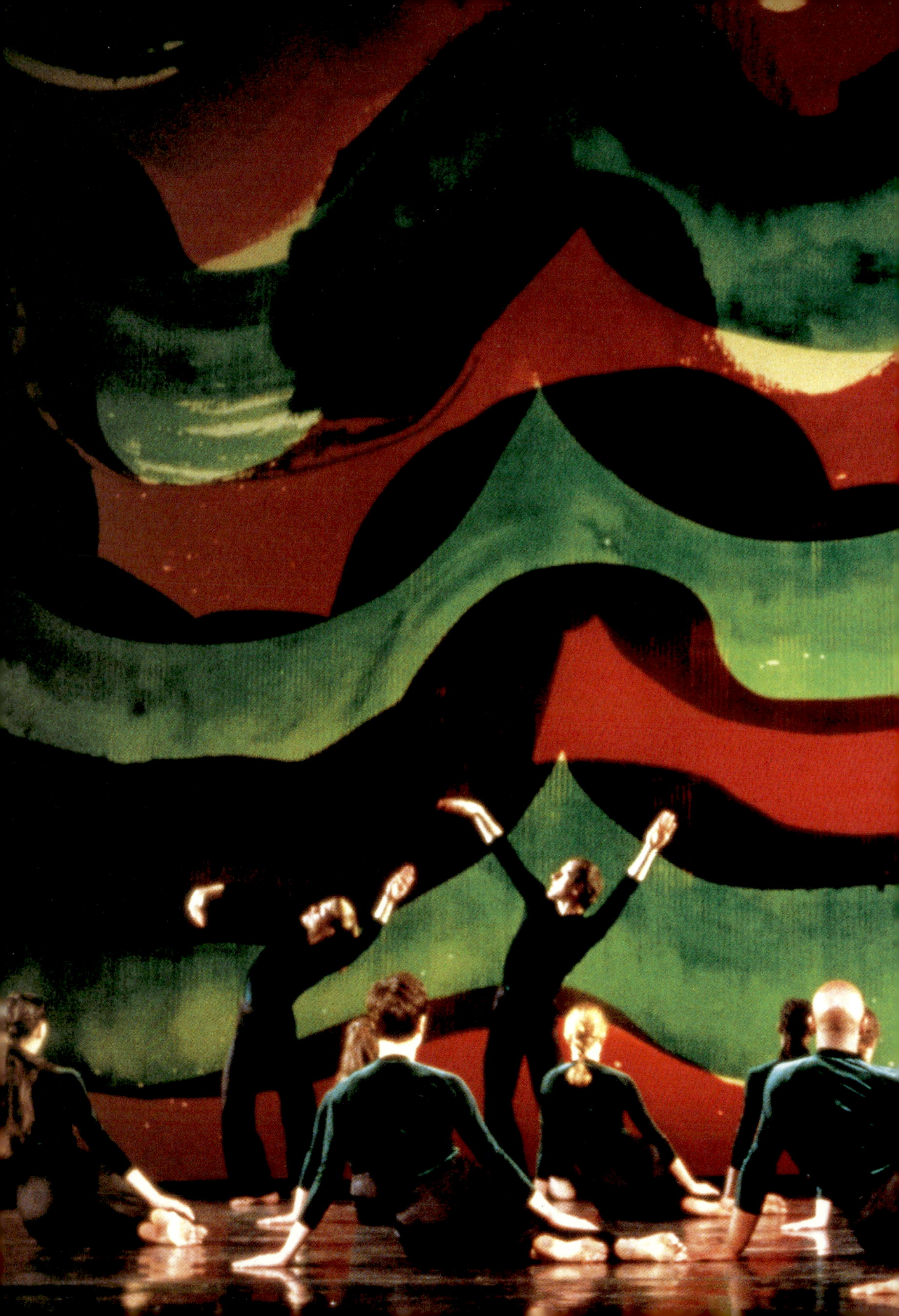

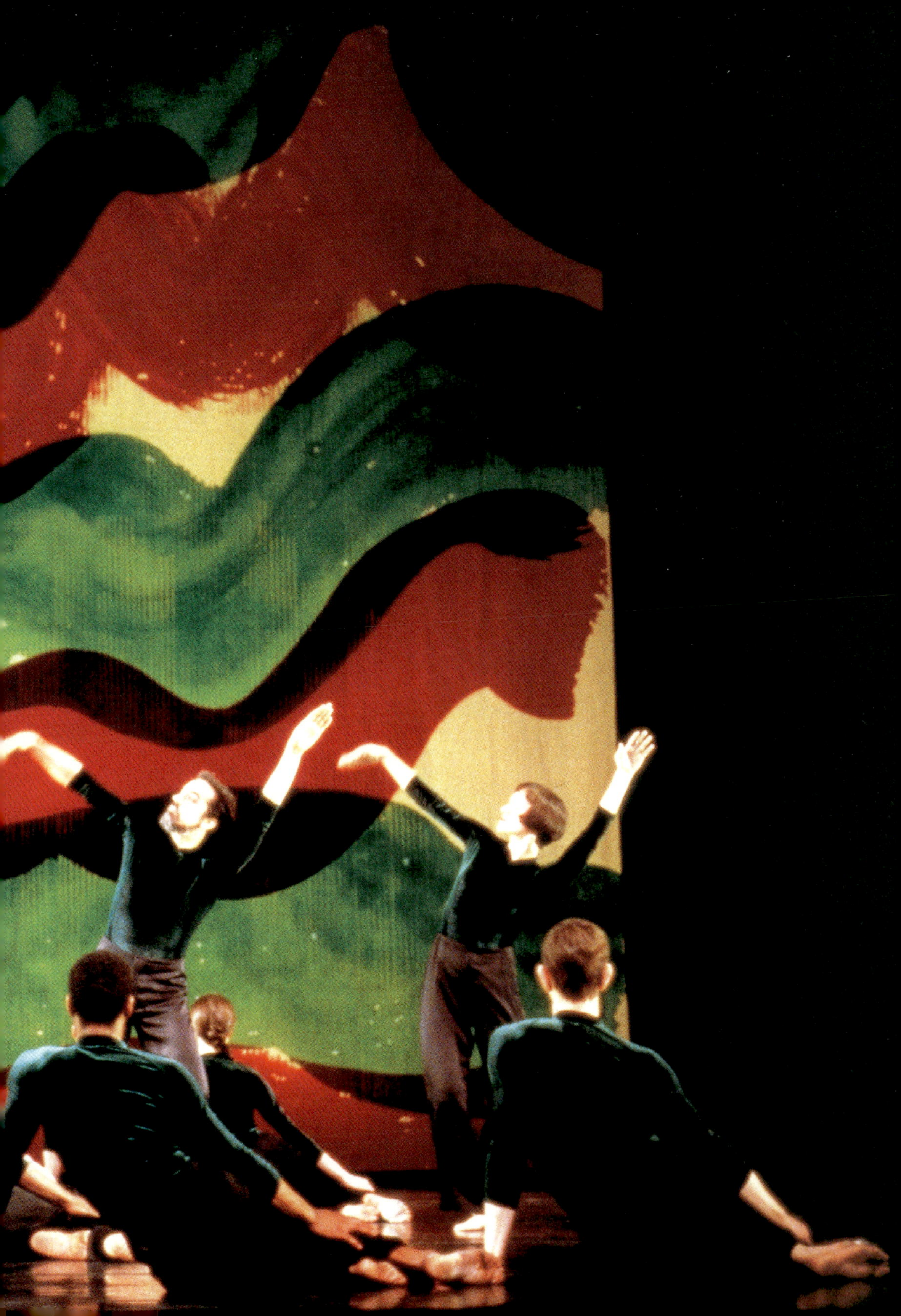

Sāvitri 1999

In a wood, at evening, in India, Death comes for Sātyavān, a woodman, throwing him and his wife Sāvitri into despair. Despite Sātyavān's attempts to resist being taken, it is Sāvitri who is able to overcome Death, sending him away empty-handed. Holst himself wrote the libretto for this short chamber opera, first performed at the Wellington Hall, London in 1916, basing it loosely on the Sanskrit story in the Mahabharata. The extreme simplicity of both narrative and orchestration is reflected in Hodgkin's striking design, which evokes a mystical combat between vision and blindness, life and death.

First performed at the Freer Gallery of Art and Arthur M. Sackler Gallery, Smithsonian Institute, Washington DC on 21 May 1999

Director	Leon Major
Set design	Howard Hodgkin
Music	Chamber opera by Gustav Holst. Conducted by Christopher Kendall
Lighting	Neil Fleitell
Photo of performance	Courtesy Freer Gallery of Art and the Arthur M. Sackler Gallery, Smithsonian Institute, Washington DC

Back cloth design for *Sāvitri*, 1999
Gouache on card, 56.5 × 81.3 cm / 22¼ × 32 ins

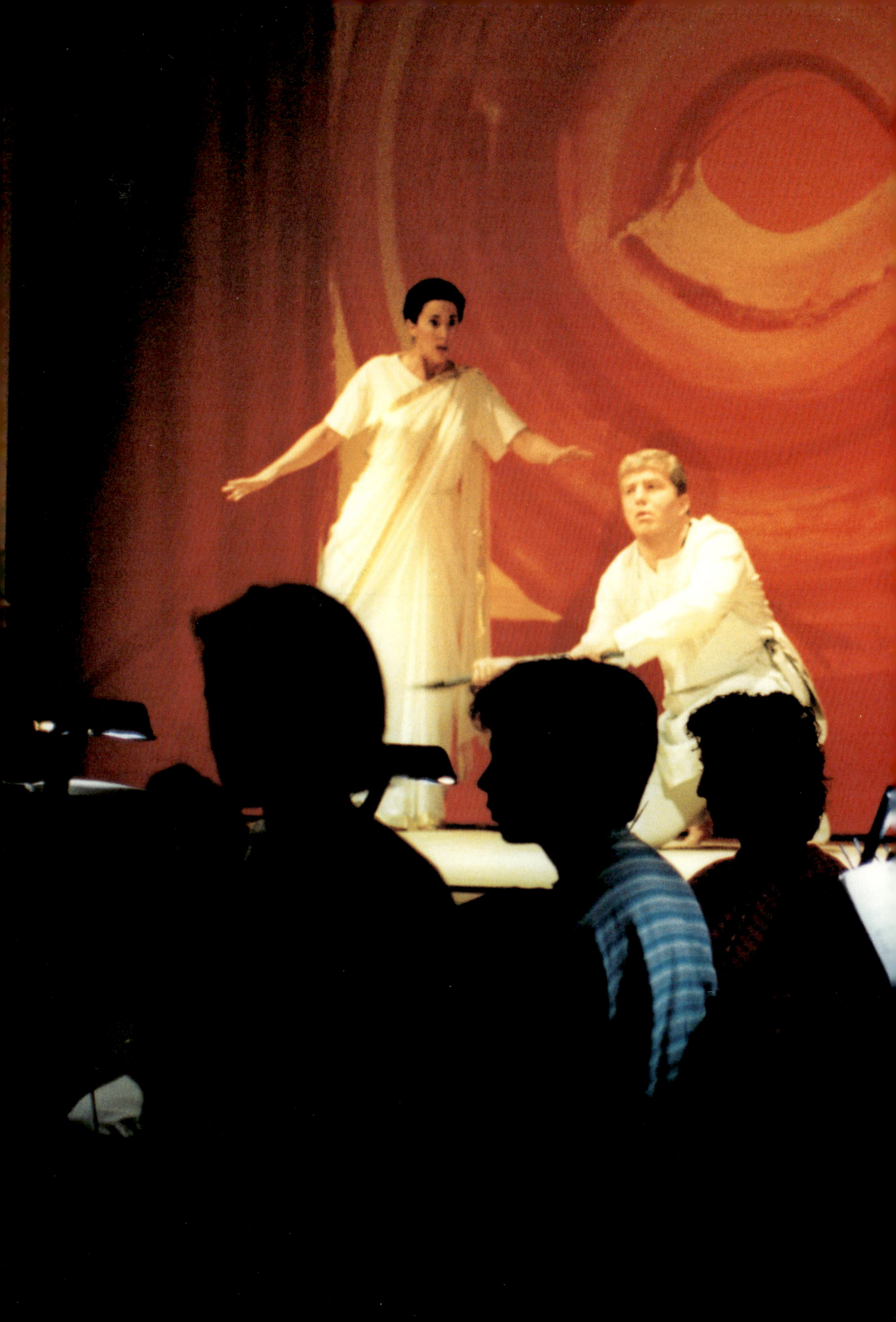

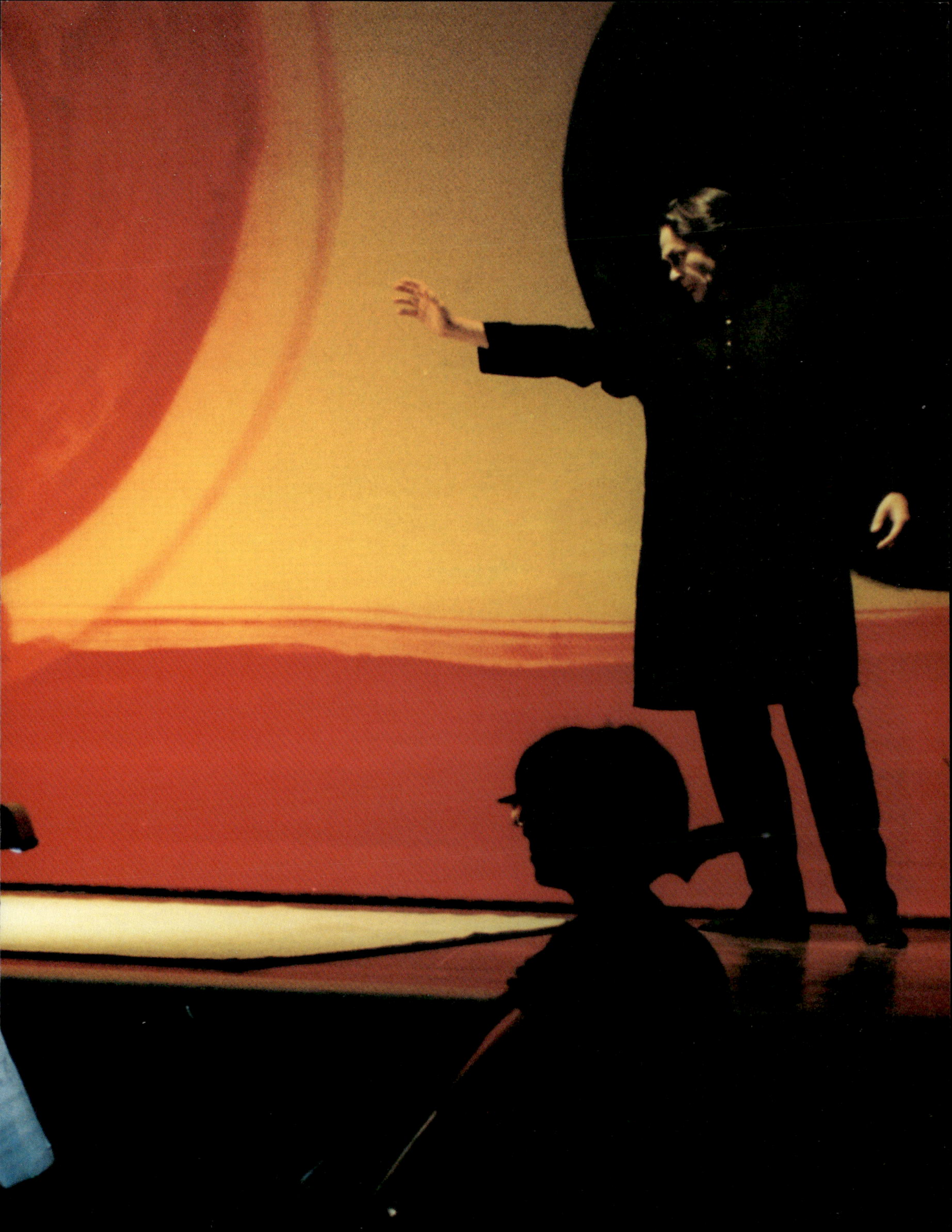

Kolam 2002

'Kolam' refers both to a tradition of painting, using powders and rice paste to trace complex, colourful geometric designs, and a form of dance popular in Sri Lanka, in which masks represent human and animal characters who tell popular folk stories. Both dance and painting form part of a good luck ritual, and, in the case of Kolam painting, transcend caste and religion. The music was commissioned from the virtuoso tabla player Zakir Hussain and the classical/jazz pianist Ethan Iverson by The Silk Road Project Inc., an ambitious global project initiated by the cellist Yo-Yo Ma to explore links between Eastern and Western cultures. Kolam was the second collaboration between Howard Hodgkin and the Mark Morris Dance Group. Morris's choreography incorporated yoga positions, movements from Kathak dance and whirling dervish turns. An initial focus on solo work turned to more complex group patterns, and a finale movement that evoked a Broadway chorus line. The backdrop, more complex than other designs by Hodgkin, was integrally related to the choreography. The distinction between the space behind and above the dancers inspired a sequence in silhouette, while spatial divisions on stage echoed its asymmetrical central line.

First performance by the Mark Morris Dance Group at Zellerbach Hall, University of California, Berkeley on 19 April 2002

Choreography	Mark Morris
Set design	Howard Hodgkin
Costume design	Katherine McDowell
Music	Zakir Hussein and Ethan Iverson
Lighting	Michael Chybowski
Photo of performance	Susana Millman
	Courtesy Mark Morris Dance Group

Back cloth design for *Kolam*, 2002
Acrylic and oil on card, 25 × 45.8 cm / 9¾ × 18 ins

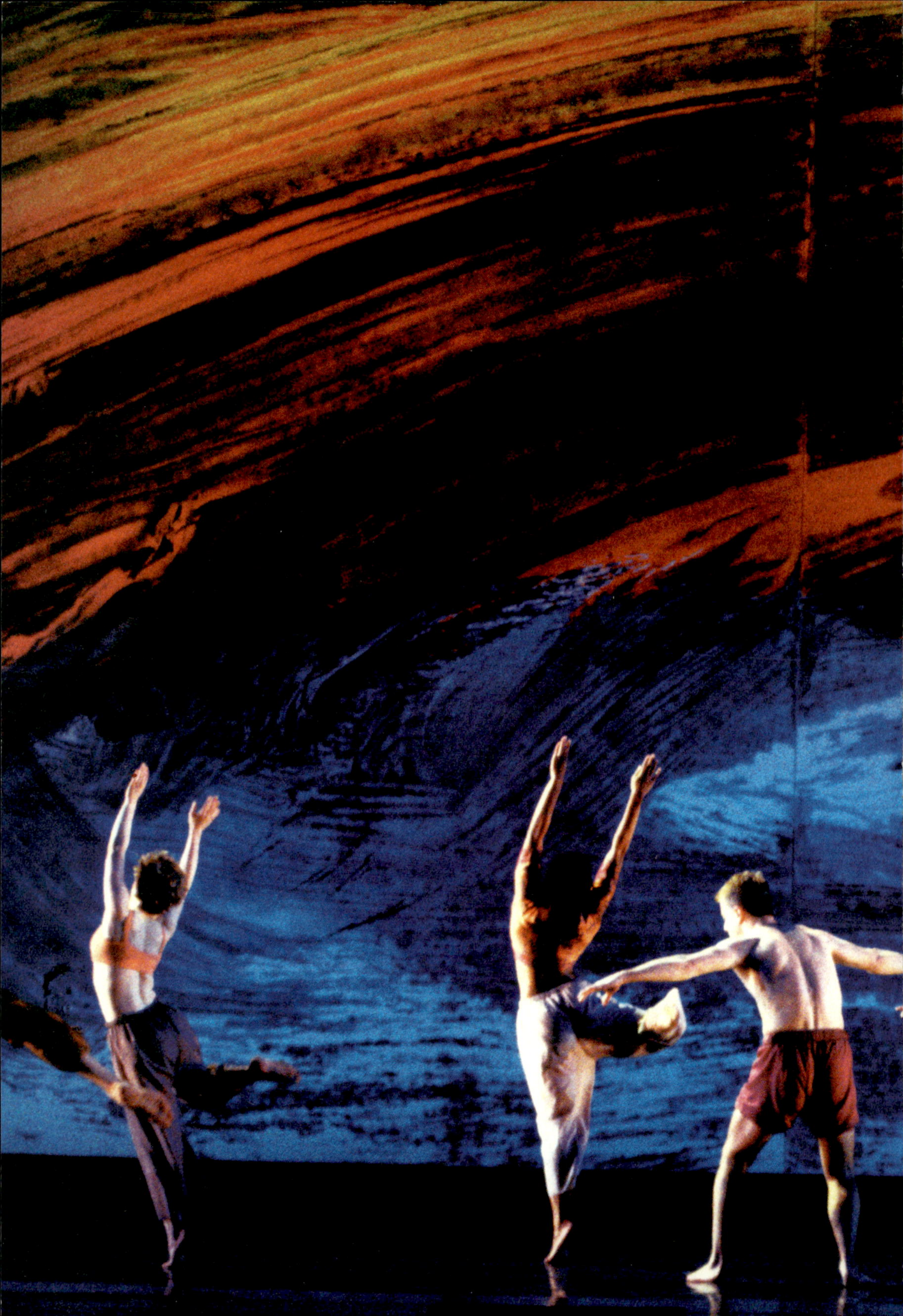

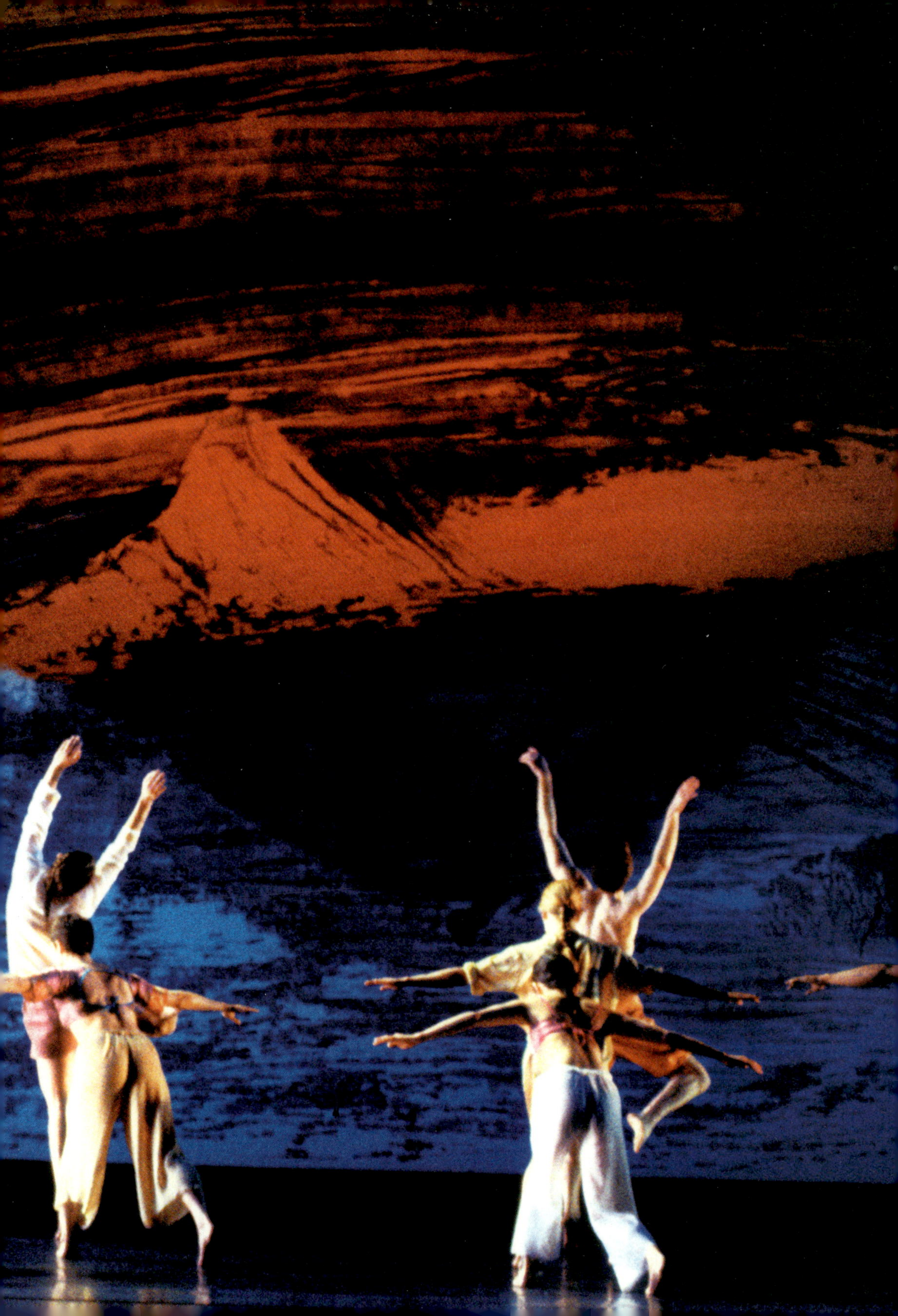

Back cloth design for *Night Music*, 1981
Water based paint and collage on paper
30.9 × 45.8 cm / 12⅛ × 18 ins
Collection Theatre Museum, London
Courtesy V&A Picture Library

Drop cloth design for *Pulcinella*, 1986
Gouache and collage on paper
44.5 × 80.7 cm / 17½ × 31¾ ins
Private Collection

Back cloth design for Act I of *Pulcinella*, 1986
Gouache and collage on paper
30.5 × 56.5 cm / 12 × 22¼ ins
Private Collection

Back cloth design for Act II of *Pulcinella*, 1986
Gouache and collage on paper
30.5 × 56.5 cm / 12 × 22¼ ins
Private Collection

Back cloth design for Act III of *Pulcinella*, 1986
Gouache and collage on paper
30.5 × 56.5 cm / 12 × 22¼ ins
Private Collection

Poster design for *Pulcinella*, 1986
Mixed media and collage on coloured paper
77.6 × 51.5 cm / 30⅝ × 20¼ ins
Private Collection

Back cloth design for Act I of *Pulcinella*, 1986
(not used)
Gouache and collage on paper
47.7 × 79.4 cm / 18¾ × 31¼ ins
Private Collection

Drop cloth design for *Pulcinella*, 1986
(not used)
Mixed media on paper relief
46.3 × 59.6 cm / 18¼ × 23½ ins
Private Collection

Back cloth design for Act I of *The Nutcracker
The Orphanage*, 1992 (not realised)
Gouache and crayon on paper
39.7 × 61.9 cm / 15¼ × 24⅜ ins
Private Collection

Back cloth design for Act II of *The Nutcracker The Land of Snow*, 1992 (not realised)
Gouache and oil paste on card
38.1 × 53 cm / 15 × 20⅞ ins
Private Collection

Back cloth design for Act III of *The Nutcracker The Land of Sweets*, 1992 (not realised)
Gouache, pencil and collage on card
37.2 × 58.4 cm / 14⅝ × 23 ins
Collection Mr and Mrs Reg Gadney

Back cloth design for *Piano*, 1989
Oil on paper mounted on board
45.7 × 55 cm / 18 × 21⅝ ins
Private Collection

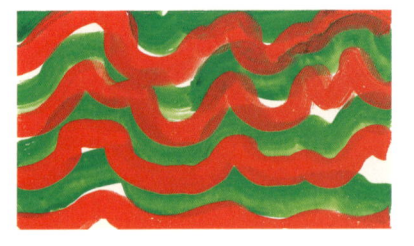

Back cloth design for *Rhymes with Silver*, 1997
Gouache on card
29.2 × 50.8 cm / 11½ × 20 ins
Private Collection

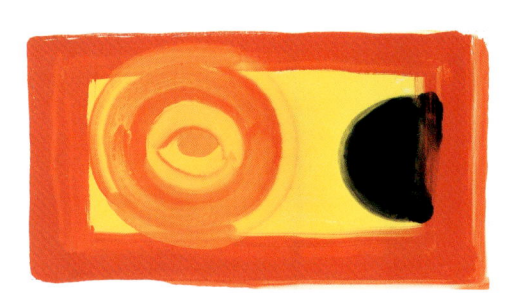

Back cloth design for *Sāvitri*, 1999
Gouache on card
56.5 × 81.3 cm / 22¼ × 32 ins
Private Collection

Back cloth design for *Kolam*, 2002
Acrylic and oil on card
25 × 45.8 cm / 9¾ × 18 ins
Private Collection

Published by Anthony d'Offay
on the occasion of the exhibition
Howard Hodgkin: Stage Designs
8–23 June 2002
Peter Pears Gallery, Aldeburgh

100 copies signed by the Artist

With thanks to Antony Peattie, John-Paul Stonard,
Jonathan Reekie, Peter B. Willberg, James Gordon,
William Jackson, Mr and Mrs Reg Gadney, Mark Morris,
The Theatre Museum, Tricia Guild and
Patrick Kinmonth who curated the exhibition.

Copyright © Anthony d'Offay, 2002
Works of art © Howard Hodgkin, 2002
Text © John-Paul Stonard, 2002

ISBN 0-947564-87-X

Design Peter B. Willberg
Co-ordination Joanna Thornberry
Photography Sue Adler, Catherine Ashmore,
Anthony Crickmay,
Prudence Cuming Associates, London
Ken Friedman and Susana Millman
Printing Offizin Scheufele, Stuttgart, Germany

Anthony d'Offay, Dering Street, London W1
Telephone +44(0)20 7499 4100
Facsimile +44(0)20 7493 4443
Email gallery@doffay.com
www.doffay.com

Cover: Fabric for costumes designed by Howard Hodgkin
for *Pulcinella,* 1987. Courtesy Designers Guild
Pages 6 and 7: Howard Hodgkin with the set design for *Piano,* 1989
Photograph Sue Adler. Courtesy The Observer
Previous page: Design for Glyndebourne Souvenir Programme, 1997
Gouache and collage on card, 39.8 × 56.2 cm / 15 $\frac{5}{8}$ × 22 $\frac{1}{8}$ ins
Private Collection